New Beginnings
Adult Coloring Bible Study

Contents

Introduction 5

Meet the Writers 6

Why Our Studies Work 8

Reflective Bible Study 9

Our Goal 10

Our Love-Directed Approach 11

S.O.A.P. (Scripture, Observation, Application, Prayer) 12

Small Group Study 16

Example Schedule 17

Hospitality Ideas 18

Directions 19

Suggested Art Supplies 21

Art Examples 22

Additional Resources 23

Lesson One 25

Art Tutorial Lesson One 37

Lesson Two 41

Art Tutorial Lesson Two 51

Lesson Three 57

Art Tutorial Lesson Three 68

Lesson Four 71

Art Tutorial Lesson Four 80

Lesson Five 85

Art Tutorial Lesson Five 94

Bonus Art Tutorial for Cover Image 100

Small Scripture Art for Tracing 105

Introduction

Bible Stories from the Heart incorporates reading, writing, and artwork to help you meditate and pray over God's scripture in a deep and meaningful way.

There is a reason we spend several days over the same scripture. Our Bible study is written as a way to deepen your comprehension and enhance your daily quiet time with God. It is our goal for you to savor God's word, not rush through it. We want each of you to take the time to FEEL God's love.

The study is designed to complete either with a small group or as an independent study. As an independent study, you are free to work at your own pace.

You may complete the study in a few days, a few weeks, or maybe months. ALL ARE GOOD. The important thing is you go deeper with GOD to let HIM fill your heart.

Feel free to invite a few friends to join you, or complete this study alone. Either way...Get prepared for some amazing God moments through this amazing Bible study!

We would love for you to participate in our Bible Stories from the Heart group on Facebook. There, you can share your artwork, fellowship with others doing our studies and participate in our regular online studies as well. Just enter **Bible Stories from the Heart** in the Facebook search bar or use the link below:

https://www.facebook.com/groups/1447039392265675/

If you would like to purchase additional pdf files of our studies for small group use, they can be found at www.biblestoriesfromtheheart.com.

Important: if you would like to be notified of future publications and receive regular devotions, please sign up for our free email club by visiting our website: www.biblestoriesfromtheheart.com.

Thank you for joining us!

Meet the Writers

Two women write the lessons from their own hearts: Leslie Eaton and Nicole Plymesser Nelson. Each has a distinct role and way for you to interact with the weekly scriptures.

 LESLIE EATON - Leslie will lead you through the reading and study of each lesson. She has over 20 years of experience as a professional educator. Ten of those years she served as a reading comprehension specialist. Leslie has undergone extensive training in both reading comprehension and effective learning strategies. She is now excited to bring these successful strategies to this study. Her goal is to empower people as they seek to experience God's love on a deeper level. She has led various Christian small groups and book studies in and around the Atlanta area for over 5 years. Now she is bringing her knowledge of teaching and her love of God's Word to Bible Stories from the Heart.

What to expect from Leslie:

You will be lead through each scripture lesson with one goal in mind - to know and understand God's love for you!

What we will do:

- Read Scriptures that are listed
- Reflect on the key verses contained in each lesson
- Answer discussion questions found with each lesson

What we will learn:

- Meaning of key words
- Relevant Biblical history
- Connection to our lives today

 NICOLE PLYMESSER NELSON - Nicole has been teaching art for 20 years—in elementary and high schools, retail settings, private lessons, and workshops. All along she has written her own curriculum that works for all ages and abilities. Nicole also has a successful illustration business that showcases her faith. She designs the illustrations for the studies so that all audiences will feel comfortable using art to study God's Word.

What to expect from Nicole:

The goal is for you to use art methods to meditate, pray and connect with God on an even deeper level - taking time to create will allow God to flow through your hands and fingers as you ALLOW HIS WORDS to INSPIRE YOU! As you work, pray over the images and words. Brain science shows that creating artwork actually creates more connections in the brain, making information easier to remember. You will be amazed at how this transforms your study and recall of the lessons!

Three options are available for you:
- Read the scriptures and create your own design in your Bible or journal.
- Use the coloring page versions - adding color in your media of choice.
- Or use the mini versions to trace into your Bible or faith art journal.

Why Our Studies Work

The Bible is a Book of LOVE.

If we are not careful, we may neglect to see God's Love in the scriptures that we read. At Bible Stories from the Heart we never want this to happen. It is our goal to view every word found in the Bible as a piece of a love letter written especially for us. Because of this, we are very intentional in the way that we write and pace both our lessons and art activities.

The devotions we will be studying will move us very slowly through certain passages of the Bible. In each lesson we will spend time reading and reflecting upon key words found in our focus verses. Doing this will help us to actually relate God's Word to our life and help us to feel His love on a much deeper level.

We believe that the BEST way to study God's Word and REALLY absorb it is to really take the time to reflect upon it and then allow it to flow THROUGH you as you read!!

LOVE is a verb - it is ACTION… it is not STAGNANT!!!

Consider for a minute the difference between the Dead Sea and the Sea of Galilee. Life does not exist in the Dead Sea, yet The Sea of Galilee THRIVES. What is the major difference between these two bodies of water is that - The Dead Sea has NO outlet and no action!

We must remember this fact and apply it whenever we spend time with the Lord.

One way to allow God's LOVE to flow through you as you study the Bible is to DOODLE or COLOR as you read.

There is something very powerful about reflecting and creating while reading.

Reflective Bible Study

About this study:

Each week we will focus on a different scripture. This scripture will then be re-read several times over that week. The purpose behind re-reading scripture is so that we will intentionally spend time reflecting and meditating on God's deep and powerful love for us.

At Bible Stories from the Heart, we believe that we should **meditate on the Word of God DAILY.**

We believe that the Word of God should be *savored* not gulped. We know that the concepts in each verse are given to us from the Holy Spirit himself! They are meant to *guide us* and *change us.* It is up to us to actually allow that to happen. We believe that in order to read God's Word as intended, we must be intentional and actually *MEDITATE* on its concepts.

David learned this in his life as did Joshua:

Psalms 119:15-16 (NKJV)
I will meditate on Your precepts and regard Your ways. I shall delight in Your statutes; I shall not forget Your word.

Joshua 1:8 (NKJV)
This Book of the Law shall not depart from your mouth, but you shall meditate in it day and night, that you may observe to do according to all that is written in it.

Our Goal

Our goal at Bible Stories from the Heart is to help you establish a deep and loving relationship with our Savior. Relationships are intentional! The best relationships develop slowly over time.

As we continue in this study, we do not want to rush through the lessons. Let's intentionally take our time and enjoy every moment that we spend in the presence of the Lord! Let's remember that we are building a relationship, not earning a grade. So, let's just relax and enjoy the journey!

How can we build a deeper relationship with Christ?

Consider this:

When you first meet a new friend or co-worker do you automatically trust this person? Of course not! Trust is something that is built and grows over time. The more time you spend with a person, the more time trust has to grow. As you spend time together, this new person will have various opportunities to display their loyalty, honesty, and abilities to you. If enough of these qualities are displayed, trust begins to grow. Then every time you notice these qualities displayed again, trust grows deeper.

It is the same with God. Authentic trust is built over time. To build this trust, we must take the time to observe and discover the true character of God.

We can accomplish this by using two simple strategies:

1. Intentional Bible Study (searching for God's love)

2. Reflective Journal Writing (reflecting on God's love / S.O.A.P.)

Our Love-Directed Approach

Intentional Bible Study

Bible study which intently looks for the character traits of God is vital.

God is LOVE! God never changes! He is and will ALWAYS be LOVE!

So, what exactly is love?

1 Corinthians 13:4-8
4 Love suffers long and is kind; love does not envy; love does not parade itself, is not puffed up; 5 does not behave rudely, does not seek its own, is not provoked, thinks no evil; 6 does not rejoice in iniquity, but rejoices in the truth; 7 bears all things, believes all things, hopes all things, endures all things. 8 Love never fails.

LOVE-Directed Bible Study Strategy:

Read each verse of the Bible with a specific purpose - To see LOVE!

If we focus on this, we will see that EVERYTHING God has ever done or will EVER do; he does out of his intense LOVE for his children.

Wherever there is LOVE- there is God!

S.O.A.P. (Scripture, Observation, Application, Prayer)

Reflective Journal Writing

(the SOAP reflection sheets in this workbook are perfect for this!)

Example

The following scripture in this example is not in this study. It has been chosen simply as an example.

SOAP Reflection (Scripture)

(S) Scripture:

Exodus 14:13-14 (NKJV)
13 And Moses said to the people, "Do not be afraid. Stand still, and see the salvation of the Lord, which He will accomplish for you today. For the Egyptians whom you see today, you shall see again no more forever. 14 The Lord will fight for you, and you shall hold your peace."

SOAP Reflection (Observation)

(O) Observation:

As a result of bad choices made by the Israelites, they were taken as slaves in Egypt for several years. After receiving word from God to do so, the Israelites are attempting to escape from their Egyptian captives. The Israelites are scared. They know that if they are caught they will be tortured or even killed for their rebellion.

I observe GOD'S LOVE in this verse! Moses is telling the Israelites to not be afraid, to stand firm, and that God will deliver them from their enemies. God is willing and able to lead them to safety - this is LOVE!

This verse PROVES that God was willing and able to rescue his children from hardships. Since God NEVER changes, he is still able and willing to rescue each of us today!

Let's use this verse to help us GROW stronger spiritual roots! Our goal throughout this study is going to be to ANCHOR our spirits deeper and deeper into God's AMAZING LOVE!

This strong anchor will help us stand firm when any future strong winds blow.

SOAP Reflection (Application)

(A) Application:

Just like the Israelites I made some bad choices in the past which led me into captivity. Unlike the Israelites, my captivity was more mental than physical. My mental captivity was a result of a past affair and other bad choices which surrounded that affair. As a result of these bad choices, Satan was able to temporarily bind me! During and even after the fallout from my affair, the devil worked to convince me that I was an evil person who was unworthy of love.

Even though I knew that God had forgiven me, Satan tried to keep me captive to my past. For a while I felt trapped in self - loathing! Eventually through my pain I reached out to God. I began reading and studying the Word of God like I never had before.

I had read the Bible in the past, but this time was different. This time when I read scripture I was actually reading for a purpose. My goal was to see if I was indeed unlovable!

What God revealed to me was the EXACT opposite! God LOVED me more than I could ever even begin to understand. Through the blood of Christ, my past sin would not keep me shut off from his love!

This was so beautiful to me! God used water to rescue the Israelites and he used BLOOD to rescue me! I began to feel lovable again. I found that the more time I spent in God's Word the less I felt trapped in my past.

Eventually I felt totally free! God RELEASED me!

All my Lord needed was for me to grow DEEP roots in his LOVE. Then he did the rest. Now God's LOVE is able to both FILL me and FLOW through me! I now know that I am indeed LOVED!

I am now able to both receive true love and to give love.

This is because God has filled me with HIS LOVE!

I now know that nothing I will do will make my Heavenly Father love me any less!

I feel so FREE! I am no longer a CAPTIVE!

SOAP Reflection (Prayer)

(P) Prayer:

Dear Lord, thank you for loving me. Thank you for forgiving me of my past sin and setting me free! Please help me to continue to grow my spiritual roots deeper and deeper into your love. Please be with me during this study. Speak to me in bold new ways. Help me to hear and respond in positive ways to your loving voice. In Jesus name I pray, Amen.

Our God ADORES each one of us! Our God is LOVE! Take a few minutes now to write your own SOAP reflection journal entry on this same verse. As we continue in this study, let's focus our hearts and minds on GOD'S AMAZING LOVE!

We encourage you to use these "LOVE-DIRECTED" Bible study strategies all throughout this study (and beyond).

Reflection Questions:

1. What am I hoping to get from this Bible Study?

2. Do I feel like I have an actual relationship with Christ? Why or why not?

3. What have I done in the past to try to build a closer relationship with God?

4. Am I willing to try a new approach to Bible Study?

Small Group Study

Example Schedule

Hours of the day can be adjusted to fit your schedule.

7:00-7:30   Snacks and social time

7:35-7:40   Open in prayer and welcome members

7:40-7:50   Encourage members to interact with the text they are about to read by underlining important words and actually writing their thoughts and questions on the lesson page as they read.

7:50-8:00   Members read the weekly lesson

8:00-8:10   Read a few of the questions and allow discussion

8:10-8:15   Get out art supplies and preview weekly art piece

8:15-9:00   Play soft music and allow time for members to meditate, pray, and create art

9:00-9:15   Share art pieces and thoughts

9:15-9:30   Pass out SOAP pages and close in prayer

Hospitality Ideas

1. Serve a light snack each week. Members can volunteer to bring finger foods or desserts on a rotating basis, if desired.

2. Offer a variety of both sugary and non-sugary drinks.

3. Have plenty of plastic cups, paper plates, as well as napkins.

4. Have name tags ready for members to fill out and wear.

5. Remember people are coming for a purpose: to connect with others and to connect with God. Be sure that all members are introduced and feel welcome.

6. Have chairs set in a circle formation to promote easy conversation throughout the lesson.

7. Provide an "ice breaker" activity for the first few meetings: there are several fun ideas found on Google (Christian small group ice breaker activities).

8. Make sure you have an area designated for the art activity. You may need to provide paper towels and plastic cups of water for watercolor paints (if needed).

9. Have a few extra boxes of crayons or colored pencils on hand in case members forget their art supplies.

Directions

To use this study in a small group setting we recommend the following:

1. As a group, meet one day per week.

2. Provide time for hospitality then open the group in prayer.

3. Each meeting will follow a set schedule:

Lesson Time:

- Introduce the lesson and have everyone open their workbooks. Give members about 10 minutes to read the lesson. Encourage everyone to jot down their thoughts directly on the lesson pages as they go.
- After the lesson is read, allow time for members to share their thoughts with the group.
- Then read a few discussion questions to the group and give time to discuss and provide collaborative feedback. Encourage everyone to participate.

Art Time:

- Allow time to get out all art supplies and preview the weekly art example. Members can choose to bring any art materials that they wish: watercolors, crayons, colored pencils, markers, etc. There is no one way to create the weekly art pieces.
- Members are encouraged to create their art in their own Faith Journal. Keeping the art pieces together is a wonderful way to document their spiritual growth and will make it easier for them to continue this process after this study ends.
- Play soft music in the background and allow members time to reflect on God's Word as they create their own art. You may recreate Nicole's piece exactly, or create any other picture that flows from them. If anyone is leery about their creativity, they may simply color one of the coloring sheets which are provided for each lesson.

Meeting Conclusion:

- The meeting will end with members sharing their art and thoughts with the group.
- Each member will leave the meeting with an understanding of how to use their SOAP reflection page. They will be encouraged to go deeper into God's Word in the next few days by reading the given scripture and then reflecting upon it.

As each week passes, it will become easier and more natural for members of the group to both reflect on, and interact with the Word of God.

Suggested Art Supplies

These are a few of Nicole's favorites but you can use any materials of your choice.

Paper: ANY kind of paper will work! Even just a basic notebook or typing paper, some may decide to do the art directly in a journaling Bible. But a separate sketchbook has several positives: you will have a book of all of your favorite verses, you can do them over and over, plus you will have space to add extra journaling as well. Canson mixed media brand is my all-time favorite due to the bright whiteness of this paper and it holds up to watercolors well.

Paints and brushes: any brand works, travel or school sets, or use the tubes of watercolor in a palette (squirt them into the pans and let them dry before use). You will want three brushes for sure: a one inch flat, a round brush, and a pointed brush.

Collage paper: Use old dictionaries from thrift stores, receipts, homework from kids, anything! Mod Podge or good old Scotch craft glue work best. Glue sticks work, but can release with watercolor on top.

Writing Utensils: There are a few different options.

- **Pen Options: Pilot G-2** in 10 for nice, black, even flow gel pen to journal and write prayers. **Sakura Black Glaze pens** or **Sharpie fine pen/markers** for outlining and large words.

- **Magic Rub Eraser** from Prismacolor.

- **Colored Pencils:** Prismacolor (artist grade) or Crayola (student grade) are your best bets depending on your budget.

Art Examples

Additional Resources

We have provided a number of additional online resources for your use.

PDF Copies of Workbooks - come in handy for those who wish to print multiple copies of the coloring pages, SOAP pages, etc. If you would like additional pdf copies of this workbook, they are available on our website. When you visit **biblestoriesfromtheheart.com**, click on the image below.

Email Club - By signing up for our email club, you will receive weekly devotions, inspirational messages, art activities and advance notification of new studies.

Video Lessons – there are video lessons for this study which can be found at: http://biblestoriesfromtheheart.net/#/newbeginningsvideos/ or you may click on the image pictured below when you visit our website.

'SAMPLE' NEW BEGINNINGS STUDY AND VIDEOS

When you visit our website, you'll also find info on our Facebook group, art tutorials, coloring pages and more: **www.biblestoriesfromtheheart.com**

Lesson One
You: A New Canvas

Scripture

John 8:1-11 (NKJV)
1 But Jesus went to the Mount of Olives. 2 Now early in the morning He came again into the temple, and all the people came to Him; and He sat down and taught them. 3 Then the scribes and Pharisees brought to Him a woman caught in adultery. And when they had set her in the midst, 4 they said to Him, "Teacher, this woman was caught in adultery, in the very act. 5 Now Moses, in the law, commanded us that such should be stoned. But what do You say?" 6 This they said, testing Him, that they might have something of which to accuse Him. But Jesus stooped down and wrote on the ground with His finger, as though He did not hear.

7 So when they continued asking Him, He raised Himself up and said to them, "He who is without sin among you, let him throw a stone at her first." 8 And again He stooped down and wrote on the ground. 9 Then those who heard it, being convicted by their conscience, went out one by one, beginning with the oldest even to the last. And Jesus was left alone, and the woman standing in the midst. 10 When Jesus had raised Himself up and saw no one but the woman, He said to her, "Woman, where are those accusers of yours? Has no one condemned you?"

*11 She said, "No one, Lord." And Jesus said to her, **"Neither do I condemn you; go and sin no more."***

Important Words

Condemn - To witness against; to show or prove to be wrong, or guilty.

Sin - hamartanó: to miss the mark, do wrong, sin

Original Word: ἁμαρτάνω
Part of Speech: Verb
Transliteration: hamartanó

No more- nothing more: nothing further

Thoughts from Leslie

Jesus gave this woman the gift of becoming a "clean canvas." She now has a fresh start to become something NEW and BEAUTIFUL!

The woman in this scripture was caught in the act of adultery. Because of her sin, she was now considered to be impure, soiled and used. Her accusers thought she was beyond repair and wanted her destroyed. Thankfully, Jesus disagreed.

We may not all be guilty of the sin of adultery, but we are all sinners. It is so incredible that just as this stained woman was given a fresh clean start, we can be given same. This second chance is provided to us through the POWERFUL blood of Jesus!

Let's take a few minutes to make some visual connections. To do this we will connect her second chance at life to refurbishing a used canvas. What others saw as stained and worthless; Jesus saw as a potential medium to hold a new creation. He was giving this woman a chance to become a beautiful masterpiece.

The adulterous woman in John was spared from death and was granted a "do-over!" All of the filth and dirt from her past sins was brushed away. She was now a CLEAN SLATE. She was free and ready to become something NEW! Incredibly, each one can receive this same wonderful gift today. We can have a FRESH START!!!

Before we can become something new and beautiful, our slate must be totally washed clean. Let's relate this to an artist painting on a canvas.

An artist will not begin to create a new piece on a used canvas without wiping it clean first. The soiled canvas must be prepared and primed before it is ready to hold a fresh new picture.

If you'll go to the Bible Stories from the Heart channel on YouTube and type **reuse a canvas step one** in the search bar; you can watch Nicole demonstrate more on this process:

Bible Stories from the Heart

| Home | **Videos** | Playlists | Channels | Discussion | About | Reuse a Canvas Step One |

Or you can use this link below:

https://www.youtube.com/channel/UCc9iQZUoqXLBWyOApHAxOvA/videos

This canvas restoration concept is the same when a person is given a fresh start.

To help us make the connections, let's consider the steps applied in the video:

1. The canvas had to be **_dusted_** off -

    Likewise, we must dust ourselves off from the "sin."

    It is necessary that we remove ourselves from the "dirt."

2. The surface of the canvas was **_sanded_** –

    This smoothed out all of the rough parts on the material's surface.

    Likewise, our "carnal" surface thinking must be sanded.

    It is vital for us to allow God's Word to change our thinking.

3. The canvas had to be **_covered_** with a primer to become a clean slate.

    Likewise, we must be covered and primed with the saving blood of Jesus in order for us to become a clean slate.

Biblical History

Before Jesus came, people were rarely given a second chance for a new life. The stains and dirt on their "canvas" was considered too filthy to clean.

Because of this, the sinners were often times killed for their crimes. Adultery was one of these "death sentence" crimes. There were many more.

Deuteronomy 22:23-24 (NKJV)
23 "If a young woman who is a virgin is betrothed to a husband, and a man finds her in the city and lies with her, 24 then you shall bring them both out to the gate of that city, and you shall stone them to death with stones, the young woman because she did not cry out in the city, and the man because he humbled his neighbor's wife; so you shall put away the evil from among you.

Big Takeaway

Jesus is waiting with open arms to give each one of us a FRESH START!

Our sins can be forgiven and we can begin our new life starting right now.

The choice is ours.

Will we choose to have a new life?

Are we ready to become a clean canvas?

Our new beautiful masterpiece of a life is waiting to begin!

Action Plan

Just as Jesus instructs this nameless woman, we must GO and SIN NO MORE.

If we are ready for our new start, we must take action.

We cannot remain in our sin.

In order to begin our New Life, we MUST leave our bad choices behind.

We must walk toward our NEW Life in Christ!

Time for Prayer

Sometimes sin can look very promising. Forbidden fruit really does seem so delicious and satisfying, but it never is! Pray to God to give you both the wisdom and the strength to know what people or choices to stay clear from. The easiest way to resist sin is to avoid it altogether. This is sometimes very difficult to do.

Pray to your Heavenly Father to guide you to take the right paths each and every day. Ask God to lead you toward HIS perfect LOVE!

Sin is NEVER the right choice! Sin will NEVER lead to LOVE!

We must be aware that even though sin can be forgiven, it always leaves behind a path of pain.

The people who were hurt through the adultery committed by the woman in John 8 still felt the consequences. The sin was forgiven, but the pain was not undone.

Discussion Questions

Numbers 6-8 are best for small groups - they can fit ALL lessons

1. When you look in the mirror, what do you see on your "canvas"?

2. What are some of your sin "smudges" that you wish could be erased?

3. Is it easy for you to believe that Jesus really can erase ALL of your sins? Why or why not?

4. If your life really was a painter's canvas, how much money would you be willing to pay in order to have it completely wiped clean?

5. Would it be easier for you to accept your fresh start if you had to pay a HUGE amount of money to receive it? Why or why not?

6. How does this particular Bible story represent God's LOVE for his children?

7. Why do you think this particular Bible story was chosen by God himself to be added into his Holy Word?

8. What is your big takeaway from this lesson?

No ~ Not Even One!

By Deborah Ann Belka

Her heart was filled with lust,
her spirit was broken down
she was sought by the men
who lived all through her town.

She lived her life in darkness,
she knew she would be stoned
yet, she carried on in her sin
till her secret was made known.

They caught her red-handed,
right in the sinful act
and they brought her to Jesus
with all the details of the fact.

They asked Him to judge her,
to indict her for her sin
they even called Him their Master
in hopes a ruling they would win.

He knew she was an adulterous,
told the blood thirsty crowd so
then He said, "You without sin"
go ahead and cast the first throw.

They caught her in her sin,
they saw the crime she had done
but they could not condemn her
no ~ not even one!

Deborah Ann Belka
Copyright 2013
https://poetrybydeborahann.wordpress.com

Bible Stories
From the Heart

Scripture: _____

_____

_____

_____

_____

_____

Observation: _____

_____

_____

_____

_____

_____

Application: _____

_____

_____

_____

_____

_____

Prayer: _____

_____

_____

_____

_____

_____

Art Tutorial Lesson One

For me, the visual that stuck out in this story was of Jesus bending down to write in the sand with all the rocks piled around Him that no one could throw. Not one of those people could throw a stone. And then to be that woman—she had probably been hiding her eyes and looking down most of the time. Her eyes would have been wide with fright, and then to see those words and the stones. Wow. So that is what I drew.

Really for such a powerful image, it is extremely simple to recreate.

1. Draw the lumpy circle shapes starting in the bottom left corner and arcing up to the top right corner. Add little pebbles in between.

2. Along that art write the first part of the verse. Then in the center of the art you created write in bubble letters go and sin no more.

3. Adding color: I used watercolors I started with the sand by adding browns and yellows. You can do this one of two ways: I just used a juicy brush on dry paper and let the two colors bleed together, but let the brush strokes stay. Or you can LIGHTLY wet the entire background and then add the browns and yellows with a juicy brush, let them mix more, and no brushstrokes.

4. When it dried I went in and added darker brown and a more golden yellow in a few places to deepen the color.

5. The rocks: I added blobs of greens—let that dry, added purple—let that dry—then blue, and finally the same with a very light grey. Letting them dry keeps them from creating weird colors by mixing and kept them vibrant on the sand.

6. Outline all the words and shapes with black marker or pen.

7. I used colored pencil to go in and highlight with scribbles in a few places to make the colors stand out even more.

Lesson Two
Dusting

Scripture

Isaiah 52:2 (NKJV)
2 Shake yourself from the dust, arise; Sit down, O Jerusalem! Loose yourself from the bonds of your neck, O captive daughter of Zion!

Important Words

Shake: shake off, out, self, overthrow, toss up and down

A primitive root (probably identical with <u>na'ar</u>, through the idea of the rustling of mane, which usually accompanies the lion's roar); to tumble about --shake (off, out, self), overthrow, toss up and down.

- Visualize the "sins" as gnats flying around you.
- It is up to us to rustle our manes and SHAKE THEM OFF!

Dust: http://www.biblemeanings.info/Words/Natural/Dust.htm

The signification of dust, is that which is damned.

- Visualize a rag after it has been used to dust a very old piece of furniture.
- This is the dust which will remain on our canvas if we do not SHAKE IT OFF!

Arise: *to leave the place or state of rest; or to leave a sitting or lying posture.*

In Biblical times, it was common for a person to sit cross legged on dirt floors.

This verse is literally instructing us to stand up out of the dust and sit down on higher ground; to literally rise up OUT of the dust.

To arise requires ACTION!

Thoughts from Leslie

Our life is like a canvas. God intended for each of us to be born as a clean, white canvas, but because we are all born with a sin nature this is not possible. Each time we act on our sin nature, our canvas becomes dusty and smudged. But, we do not need to be discarded when this happens. There is still hope for us! Thanks to Jesus, our life (canvas) can be wiped clean and refurbished! It is not too late for any of us to become something new and beautiful! Let's reflect once again on the steps required to refurbish a used canvas.

If you haven't yet watched "New Canvas" video on the Bible Stories from the Heart YouTube page, this is a great time to do so! Just type **Bible Stories from the Heart New Canvas video** in the YouTube search bar or use the link below:

https://www.youtube.com/channel/UCH7u9bDw9ZcW98egRj_iHMw

Let's take note of the first key step: Dusting

In order to hold a new picture, a canvas must first be dusted.

Metaphorically speaking, we must allow the same. We must allow the dirt to be removed from our lives before we can hold a new "life picture". Allowing Jesus to rid us from the dust of sin is sometimes difficult, but ALWAYS necessary. Before we can allow Him to clean us, we **must** *first* be willing to stand up **out of the sin.** This can be quite difficult to do. **It requires us to first see ourselves as a dirty canvas!**

Action Plan

Let's write down all of the sins we wish to release. We should not leave ANY SIN out, no matter how big or how small.

Before we begin, let's pray to God to help us write this list.

To make this have a deeper impact, let's write each sin using a black marker.

Let's use a crisp clean white piece of paper (or canvas).

After we make our list, let's smudge the ink from our writing and scribble over our paper (or canvas) to make it look dirty and soiled.

Sin is filth!

It is vital for us to SEE it as such!!

Big Takeaway

In order to become a beautiful new masterpiece, we must first take the necessary steps of preparation. Nothing will change on our "picture" unless we first dust off our canvas. Unless we remove the dust first we are simply wasting our time and energy. Fresh paint will not stick to dusty surfaces!!! Removing the dust is going to require more strength than we possess on our own.

This step requires intentionally keeping a dust rag in your back pocket.

For us, our "dust rag" is The Word of God!

It is vital for each one of us to draw on the mite of God to guide and empower us each and every day. God loves us so deeply! He is ready and willing to help, *but we must rely on Him DAILY!*

Prayer

Pray for God to give you clear vision, wisdom and strength. Sin is often disguised as beauty. Because of this, it is vital for God to show us the TRUE ugliness of sin. We must ask our Heavenly Father to guide us with *new eyes*. God is willing, able, and WAITING to help us every step of the way, but we must rely on Him daily! We must rid our lives of the DUST!

We need God's help!!!!!!

Discussion Questions

1. Are there some sins that are easier for you to "dust off" than others? If so, what makes some easier?

2. Does it sometimes seem easier to remain sitting in the "dust" than to stand up out of it? If so, why?

3. Sometimes we sit in the dust for so long that our spiritual legs seem to fall asleep. If this happens we need the help of a strong Christian friend to pull us up. Do you have a friend you could turn to if needed?

4. Would it be easy for you to accept their help? Why or why not?

A Mop and A Broom
By Deborah Ann Belka

I wander through my mind,
go from room to room
and in each one I find
a mop and a broom.

In the room of transgression,
with all its dirt and grime
I sweep away all my sins
He washes away my crime.

In the room of worry,
with all its anxious fears
I sweep away my concerns
He washes away my tears.

In the room of sorrow,
with all the loss I've known
I sweep away my grief,
He washes away my groan.

In the room of troubles,
with all its weight and pain
I sweep away my faults
He washes away the stain.

In the room of doubt,
with every regret and qualm
I sweep away my disbelief
He washes me with His calm.

Bible Stories
From the Heart

Scripture: _____
_____
_____
_____
_____
_____

Observation: _____
_____
_____
_____
_____
_____

Application: _____
_____
_____
_____
_____
_____

Prayer: _____
_____
_____
_____
_____
_____

Art Tutorial Lesson Two

Leslie knew exactly what she wanted for this art piece. I was leery—I don't draw animals very often! But I do draw motion! And drawing this lion in action made the piece easy. I have included step by step very detailed directions on how to draw the lion. Painting is very straight forward, nothing exciting this time since the drawing itself takes center stage. Here is the finished piece:

And following are my tracings and notes to walk you through the process.

No worries! You will do great!

You'll see how to draw him on the next page.

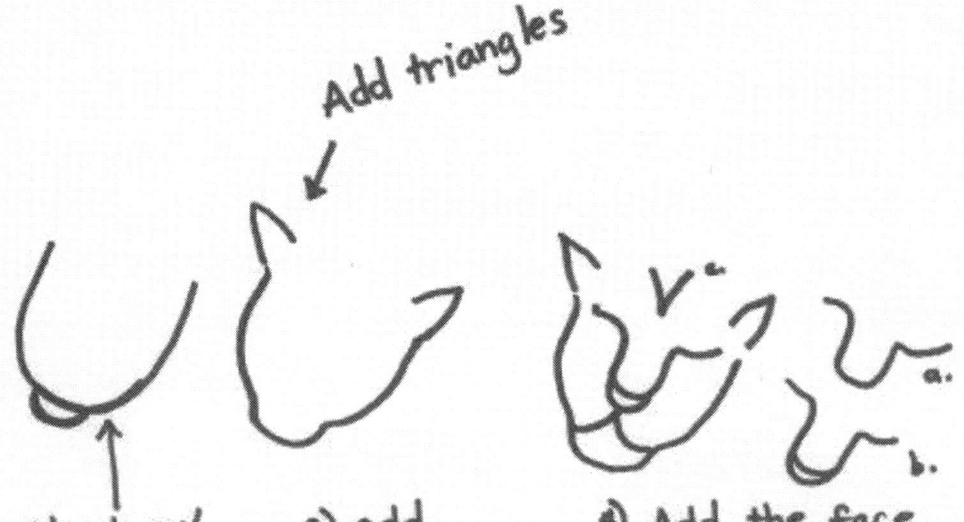

Add triangles

1) start w/
a U angled
to 1 side

2) add another
smaller U shape
to the bottom as
a "chin"

3) add
ears
& erase
"chin" line
in the middle

4) Add the face
a. U just like
a cursive U ☺
b. add a bump
at the bottom
for the base
of the nose.
c. add a V on
the forehead

a.

b.

5) Add the mane with curving triangle/v lines - go all the way around

6) add 4 lines coming down for the legs
* if it helps make the left leg by drawing this shape & then add the other leg.

7) fill in the round body between the head & legs

shake yourself from the dust; ARISE

Isaiah 52:2a

Lesson Three
<u>Sanding</u>

Scripture

Ephesians 4:17-24 (NKJV) The New Man (or for this lesson: The NEW Canvas)
17 This I say, therefore, and testify in the Lord, that you should no longer walk as the rest of the Gentiles walk, in the futility of their mind, 18 having their understanding darkened, being alienated from the life of God, because of the ignorance that is in them, because of the blindness of their heart; 19 who, being past feeling, have given themselves over to lewdness, to work all uncleanness with greediness.

*20 But you have not so learned Christ, 21 if indeed you have heard Him and have been taught by Him, as the truth is in Jesus: 22 that you **put off**, concerning your former conduct, the old man which grows corrupt according to the deceitful lusts, 23 and **be renewed** in the spirit of your mind, 24 and that you put on the new man which was created according to God, in true righteousness and holiness.*

Important Words

put off - To lay aside.

be renewed - To renovate; to restore to a former state, or to a good state, after decay or depravation; to rebuild; to repair.

Thoughts from Leslie

Our life is like a canvas. We are all born with a clean, white canvas. Over time sin causes our canvas to become rough and dusty. But, like a painter's canvas, our lives can be wiped clean and smoothed again! It is not too late for any of us to become something new and beautiful!

Let's reflect again on the steps required to refurbish a used canvas. Watch the "New Canvas" video to get a great visual of this process:

https://www.youtube.com/watch?v=a2H6AKzZCKY

Let's take note of the second key step

Sanding

In order to hold a new picture, a canvas must first be sanded. Physically we must do the same. We must remove the callouses and rough edges from our lives before we can hold a new "life picture". Smoothing ourselves from the rough edges caused from sin is sometimes difficult, but ALWAYS necessary. Before we take any other steps, we **must** *first* be in total agreement with our Heavenly Father.

This can sometimes be difficult to do. *It requires changing our thinking!* *We must intentionally smooth out our jagged thoughts and totally align them with our creator.*

To accomplish this, we will need wisdom that we do not possess on our own. We will need to refer to God's Holy Word, to help us.

The Bible is our sandpaper!

Sanding is necessary because it is the step which will restore our minds back into agreement with our Heavenly Father. The old lies and misconceptions that are roughing up our thoughts must be smoothed out and removed.

Big Takeaway

We have seen from our focus video that a used canvas can be transformed into a new masterpiece. But it must first be renewed.

This renewal begins with a dusting process, but it does not end there.

Sanding of the canvas must occur next. After the initial surface dirt is removed through dusting, the material must be altered on a deeper level. Sanding forces the rough edges to be removed. This step leaves the canvas smooth and aligned. The used canvas is then one step closer to holding a beautiful new masterpiece.

For us to become something new and beautiful, we must also experience this necessary second refurbishing step.

After we dust our surface and leave our sins behind, we must then be sanded. This second step will help us not return to our past sins. To be fully sanded, we must spend quality time reading the Word of God. God's Love and Truth is what we need to align us! In other words, The Bible is to us what sandpaper is to an artist.

Action Plan

The Word of God cannot change us UNLESS we spend time reading it. If we truly desire to become a new and beautiful creation, we must first take action! We must spend time immersed in the Word of God. To help accomplish this, we strongly encourage you to create a reading plan.

Because we all learn and study differently, our plans do not have to be identical. There is no one right way to read the Bible. The most important thing is that we allow our hearts and minds to become totally immersed in the truths we read as we study.

To help us accomplish this, spend time reflecting on a verse or two each time you. By taking time to reflect, we are allowing our brain to fully process and interact with the words on the page. It is this interaction that changes our thought patterns. This reflection piece can add a whole new dimension to our daily studies.

One way to reflect is to create pictures as you read. Another way is to take notes. A third way is to ask questions along the way. The possibilities are limitless, but this reflection step is very needed.

If you do not have a set way that you like to reflect as you read, I suggest that you try all of the suggestions which are added in this study.

1. Color the picture included with each lesson.
2. Answer the discussion questions.
3. Complete the SOAP reflection page to interact with God's Word even more.

See which one or ones help you go deeper into your daily Bible reading. Add the ones you like to your new reading plan.

Discussion Questions

1. Why is reading God's Word on a regular basis vital in keeping our thoughts properly aligned?

2. What does your current reading plan look like in regards to reading God's Word?

3. Is it difficult for you to understand the scriptures you read? What have you done so far to help yourself comprehend?

4. Everyone learns differently. Do you know what your learning style is? Are you a visual, auditory, or tactile learner? How can knowing your style help you in your daily Bible study?

5. Did you try the reflection suggestions provided with this lesson: the coloring piece, discussion questions, reflection page? If so, which one helped you the most and why?

Here is a free quiz to determine your learning style:

http://www.educationplanner.org/students/self-assessments/learning-styles-quiz.shtml

What Is the Bible?
By Deborah Ann Belka

The Bible is the breath of God,
profitable for teaching
it's a reproof and a correction
to use for righteous training.

It's the Living Word of God,
it makes us competent and able
it equips us for good works
keeping our lives in Him stable.

It is a lamp to our feet,
a light unto our path
when we choose to follow it
it will keep us from God's wrath.

It's to be used for mediation,
all our living nights and days
it is the Bread of Life
that shows us our evil ways.

It instructs us on endurance,
encourages us in the faithful race
it persuades us to continue
to seek and find God's face.

It is living and it active,
it's as sharp as a two edge sword
it pierces through the heart
so our souls can be restored.

It's a wonder to the open eye,
out of the law comes salvation
it's the pure spiritual milk
spilling forth God's revelation.

It's to be stored in our hearts,
it will keep us from sin
it's to be used in our daily battles
so over the enemy we will win.

It will guard our hearts and minds,
it will keep us in perfect peace
and we should always keep . . .
our Bible's within close reach.

But, for some it sits on their shelf,
other's shove it in a drawer
and most just don't make the time
to read the Bible anymore!

~~~~~~~~~~~~~~

Psalm 119:11
King James Version

"Thy word have I hid in mine heart,
that I might not sin against thee."

https://poetrybydeborahann.wordpress.com

Bible Stories
From the Heart

Scripture: _____

_____

_____

_____

_____

_____

Observation: _____

_____

_____

_____

_____

_____

Application: _____

_____

_____

_____

_____

_____

Prayer: _____

_____

_____

_____

_____

_____

Art Tutorial Lesson Three

When reading this my mind immediately was renewed with IDEAS. And JOY. The composition needed to reflect those two things bursting from my head! And that is exactly what I drew!

The colors of this piece are joyful and free. No boundaries. No rules. Just pure. Emotional. Fun. New.

1. To start I drew the person at the bottom of the paper. (See next page for detailed instructions.)
2. Then I used a small plate to draw curved lines to write on starting above the head and working up.
3. Write the words of the verse using a basic print; add spirals to some letters.
4. Add the lines and circles at the top to crown the entire drawing.
5. Add color! Go wild and just have fun! Let this be a complete expression of you! **BUT be careful about what wet colors you put next to each other! Make sure they will mix to create a true color and not mud.

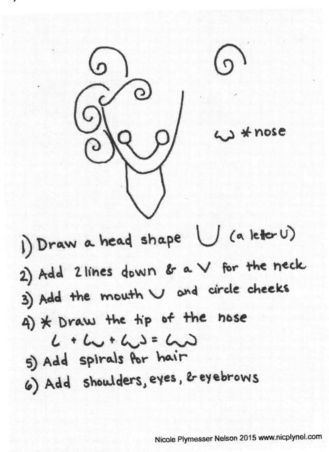

1) Draw a head shape ⋃ (a letter U)
2) Add 2 lines down & a ∨ for the neck
3) Add the mouth ⋃ and circle cheeks
4) * Draw the tip of the nose
   ⌞ + ⌣ + ⌣⌐ = ⌣⌐
5) Add spirals for hair
6) Add shoulders, eyes, & eyebrows

Nicole Plymesser Nelson 2015 www.nicplynel.com

Lesson Four
Covering

Scripture

Ephesians 1:7 (NKJV)
In Him we have redemption through His blood, *the forgiveness of sins, according to the riches of His grace.*

1 John 1:7 (NKJV)
But if we walk in the light as He is in the light, we have fellowship with one another, **and the blood of Jesus Christ His Son cleanses us from all sin.**

Important Word

Cleanses - *To purify; to make clean; to remove filth, or foul matter of any kind,* or by any process whatever, as by washing, rubbing, scouring, scraping, purging, ventilation; to cleanse the hands or face to cleanse a garment; to cleanse the bowels; to cleanse a ship; to cleanse an infected house.

It is important to note that the blood of Jesus is much better than any man-made primer. Man-made primer will only cover old mistakes. The all-powerful blood of Jesus will actually ERASE our past mistakes!

Once we are covered by Jesus, our old sins are no longer in existence. Our surface does not only appear to be clean, we literally are CLEAN down to our core

Let's consider a beautiful old hymn:

<u>Nothing but the Blood of Jesus</u>

What can wash away my sin?
Nothing but the blood of Jesus.
What can make me whole again?
Nothing but the blood of Jesus.
Oh, precious is the flow,
That makes me white as snow;
No other fount I know,

Nothing but the blood of Jesus.

For my pardon this I see,
Nothing but the blood of Jesus.
For my cleansing this my plea,
Nothing but the blood of Jesus.

Nothing can for sin atone,
Nothing but the blood of Jesus.
Naught of good that I have done,
Nothing but the blood of Jesus.

This is all my hope and peace,
Nothing but the blood of Jesus.
This is all my righteousness,
Nothing but the blood of Jesus.

There is truly NOTHING like the blood of Jesus!

In this lesson we are going to compare it to artist's *gesso,* but just to be clear, there literally is NOTHING that has or will ever be in existence that has the cleansing power of Jesus' blood!

The blood of Jesus is the only *gesso* that can ever fully cover the canvas of our life.

Thoughts from Leslie

Our life is like a canvas. We are all born with a clean, white canvas. Over time, sin causes our canvas to become dusty and smudged, and literally covered in filth. But, like a painter's canvas, our lives can be wiped clean and refurbished! It is not too late for any of us to become something new and beautiful!

Let's reflect once again on the steps required to refurbish a used canvas. Watch the "New Canvas" video to get a great visual of this process:

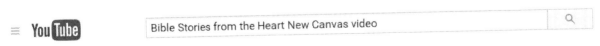

Bible Stories from the Heart New Canvas video

https://www.youtube.com/watch?v=a2H6AKzZCKY

In this lesson let's take note of the third key step

Covering

In order to hold a new picture, a used canvas must first be completely covered with a primer of some sort. Physically we must do the same. We must be completely covered before we can hold a new "life picture".

There is only ONE way to cover all of our sins and become white again, and that is through the blood of Jesus!

The blood of Jesus is our primer!

Will we choose to be covered today?

Action Plan

If you have not yet accepted Jesus as your Lord and Savior, I encourage you to do so today. Find a Christian friend or a local pastor who can lead you through the plan of salvation.

Jesus is waiting and willing to enter your heart and cover all of your sins, but you must invite Him to come in first. For those of us who already have accepted Jesus as our Lord and Savior, let's spend time in prayer today.

Jesus is willing to cover all of our sins, but FIRST we must confess and repent each one. Our Messiah will not grab sins out of our hands that we are not yet willing to give to Him. Let's spend time today releasing all of our sins to Him.

Big Takeaway

The all-powerful blood of Jesus will actually ERASE our past mistakes! Once we are covered by Jesus, our old sins are no longer in existence. Our surface does not only appear to be clean, we literally are CLEAN down to our core!

Prayer

Before our sins can be covered, we need to first release them. This is sometimes very difficult to do. Before we go further in our discussion, let's ask our Heavenly Father to give us the strength that we need to be able to release our sins to Him.

Discussion Questions

Read this verse from the hymn again slowly, questions will follow.

Nothing but the blood of Jesus

What can wash away my sin?
Nothing but the blood of Jesus.
What can make me whole again?
Nothing but the blood of Jesus.
Oh, precious is the flow,
That makes me white as snow;
No other fount I know,

Nothing but the blood of Jesus.

1. This hymn makes a point to say that **nothing but the blood of Jesus** can wash away our sins. Why do you think this hymn states that? What are other possible ways that people might try in an attempt to wash away their sins?

2. In this hymn it states that **nothing but the blood of Jesus** can make us whole again. What are other things that people may turn to to try to make them feel whole again? Do these things work? Why or why not?

3. Are there sins in our lives today that we are struggling to release to Jesus? If so, what are they? We may not be ready to confess them to others, but we can confess them to ourselves. Remember our Messiah will not grab sins out of our hands - we must be willing to release them to Him.

Cleansed

By Deborah Ann Belka

Forgiveness divine,
repent and receive
the beauty of grace
when you believe.

Bathe in His mercy,
pardoning and free
healing and restoring
until all of eternity.

Washed of your sin,
released from shame
when you trust Jesus
nothing is the same.

Healing compassion,
immersion of love
blood of the Son
a gift from above.

Forgiveness divine,
today is the day
mercy and grace
is just a prayer away!

~~~~~~~~

Bible Stories
From the Heart

Scripture: _____

_____

_____

_____

_____

Observation: _____

_____

_____

_____

_____

Application: _____

_____

_____

_____

_____

Prayer: _____

_____

_____

_____

_____

Art Tutorial Lesson Four

How do you show this without being gory??? It is such an important piece of being a Christian, of being washed clean by the sacrifice that Jesus made! But I get all sorts of queasy thinking of blood! So I will admit, I hit the internet to get some ideas.

I finally ran across an image of a fingerprint. And I thought of Jesus' hands. And I thought of Him touching me with grace and leaving His mark on me. And I knew...this was how I would portray this verse:

This might seem really detailed and daunting, but it is one of the EASIEST things I have ever drawn!

1. Start by drawing IN PENCIL one large oval. Erase a few breaks in that oval.

2. Draw a spiral line in one section of that oval—it can go anywhere. You can even mimic your own fingerprint!

3. Now—use a paintbrush FILLED with red paint. Start making random lines inside that oval that are nice and thick. Paint over the spiral, paint the oval. That is all this is! And you can't do it wrong. Add little dots and lines if you need filler. Go back over some lines if you want them darker.

4. Write the verse in black marker around the circumference of the fingerprint.

5. Add wet juicy green and blue to the outside by setting a flat brush near the words and pulling it out to the edge of the page. Green is opposite red on the color wheel and will make it pop.

6. Here is a basic shape to follow

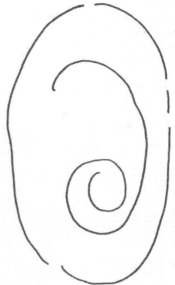

1) In pencil draw an oval – but with breaks ...or erase for breaks.
2. Add the spiral in the center.

In HIM we have REDEMPTION through HIS blood, the forgiveness of sins. Ephesians 1:7

In HIM we have REDEMPTION through HIS blood, the forgiveness of sins. Ephesians 1:7

Nicole Plymesser Nelson 2015

Lesson Five
Protecting

Scripture

Ephesians 6:10-20 (NKJV) The Whole Armor of God
10 Finally, my brethren, be strong in the Lord and in the power of His might. 11 Put on the whole armor of God, that you may be able to stand against the wiles of the devil. 12 For we do not wrestle against flesh and blood, but against principalities, against powers, against the rulers of the darkness of this age, against spiritual hosts of wickedness in the heavenly places. 13 Therefore take up the whole armor of God, that you may be able to withstand in the evil day, and having done all, to stand.

14 Stand therefore, having girded your waist with truth, having put on the breastplate of righteousness, 15 and having shod your feet with the preparation of the gospel of peace; 16 above all, taking the shield of faith with which you will be able to quench all the fiery darts of the wicked one. 17 And take the helmet of salvation, and the sword of the Spirit, which is the word of God; 18 praying always with all prayer and supplication in the Spirit, being watchful to this end with all perseverance and supplication for all the saints— 19 and for me, that utterance may be given to me, that I may open my mouth boldly to make known the mystery of the gospel, 20 for which I am an ambassador in chains; that in it I may speak boldly, as I ought to speak.

Thoughts from Leslie

Our life is like a canvas. We are each born with a clean white canvas. Over time sin causes our canvas to become smudged and filthy. Through the blood of Jesus each one of us can be restored back to a pure white state once again. Once this happens we have a second chance to become something new and beautiful!

The possibilities for our new "pictures" are beyond our wildest imaginations. We have the opportunity to become a priceless new masterpiece! Each picture God has envisioned for our lives is extraordinary and unique. Each new stroke He leads us to take will only add value to our priceless art.

Because of this, it is vital that we protect our picture every minute of every day. We must not allow the dust of evilness to destroy the beautiful art which God is guiding us to create!

To help us understand about this needed protection, let's consider how valuable art is protected. In a museum each masterpiece is contained in a thick glass box of some sort. As "living" art, we cannot live our daily lives contained in a box, but, as Christians, we have something even better! We have the ultimate protection - The all-powerful and protecting armor of God!

Important Words

Psalm 18:2 (NKJV)
2 The Lord is my rock and my fortress and my deliverer; My God, my strength, in whom I will trust; My shield and the horn of my salvation, my stronghold.

Let's look more closely at the meanings of some of the key words found in this verse. Reflecting on their power will help us truly understand the strength and mite that is within our reach- when we choose to put on the **full armor of the Lord.**

Rock - a natural refuge **(from a storm, or from an attack)**

Original Word: מַחֲסֶה
Transliteration: machaseh or machseh

Fortress - any fortified place; a fort; a castle; a strong hold; a place of defense or security.

Original Word: חֵיל
Transliteration: chel

The word fortress means a place of defense, **a place so strengthened that an enemy could not approach it**, or where one would be safe.

Deliverer - one that **saves or rescues from danger or destruction**

derived from original word *palat*: meaning to escape

Original Word: פָּלַט
Transliteration: palat

Big Takeaway

We live in an evil world. There is filth waiting around every corner ready to destroy our art. BUT....each one of us is offered the highest level of protection.

Our Heavenly Father is offering to help us.

Our Almighty God can not only keep us from danger, He can also rescue us from destruction. The choice is ours on a daily basis. We can rely on our own strength or we can choose to put on the full armor of God! What will our decision be?

Action Plan

Putting on the full armor of God requires action on our part.

To make sure we are completely covered in HIS power daily here are some steps we should take:

1. Begin each day in prayer.
2. Spend time immersed in God's Word, meditating on one or two key verses.
3. Draw upon those verses throughout your day. Write them down and carry them with you if it helps.
4. Spend every moment of your day living intentionally connected to your Heavenly Father.
5. Strive to align every action and decision you make with honesty, righteousness, and love.

These steps may not come naturally at first, but if we strive to do them each day for several weeks, they will soon become new habits for us.

New habits lead to new thinking. New thinking leads to new outcomes!!!!

Discussion Questions

1. What routines do you have first thing in the morning? Do these routines help you begin each day on a positive and energized note? Why or why not?

2. What are some new habits you would like to add into your daily routine?

3. What are some habits that you would like to remove from your daily routine?

4. What do you need to do to accomplish these new habits?

5. What would it look like for you personally to "put on" the armor of God before you leave your house each day?

Prayer

Spend some time in prayer. Ask your Heavenly Father to help guide and strengthen you. Lean on Him to help you form new positive habits, routines and thought patterns in your life on a daily basis.

Just Like Rambo

By Deborah Ann Belka

I fight the good fight,
fair and square . . .
I'm always prepared
for spiritual warfare.

I'm ready for Satan,
and his principalities
when I'm done . . .
there'll be fatalities.

I fight the good fight,
between flesh and lust
I fight because I know
winning is a must.

I'm armed and dangerous,
God's Word is my ammo
when the enemy strikes
I can be just like Rambo.

I fight the good fight,
fair and square . . .
I never lose a battle
for, God's armor I wear!

Bible Stories
From the Heart

Scripture:_____

_____

_____

_____

_____

_____

Observation:_____

_____

_____

_____

_____

Application:_____

_____

_____

_____

_____

Prayer: _____

_____

_____

_____

_____

_____

Art Tutorial Lesson Five

This was a challenging verse for me to illustrate! I struggled with do I add a person? (No—wanted it to be gender neutral.) Do I draw a cartoon? (No—needs to be strong, not cutesy.) It is a wordy verse, so what do I include? (ARMOR of GOD stood out to me—not of anything else but God, and something strong.)

So I decided on this: The words armor of God needed to be big, bold, and be the focal point. I wanted the shield, sword, and belt to be in there, but be parts of the whole—not in the fore front. I had to choose colors that wouldn't hide them or make them blend together.

And this is how I did it:

1. I started with the most important piece: the lettering of Armor of God. This drawing shows how I drew the letters. I did it in pencil, then once everything else was colored and done, I went over everything with black marker.

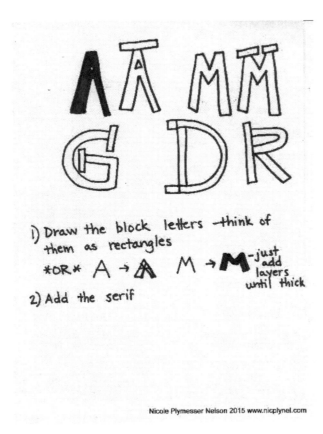

Nicole Plymesser Nelson 2015 www.nicplynel.com

94

2. Next I added the other components. Here is how I drew them:

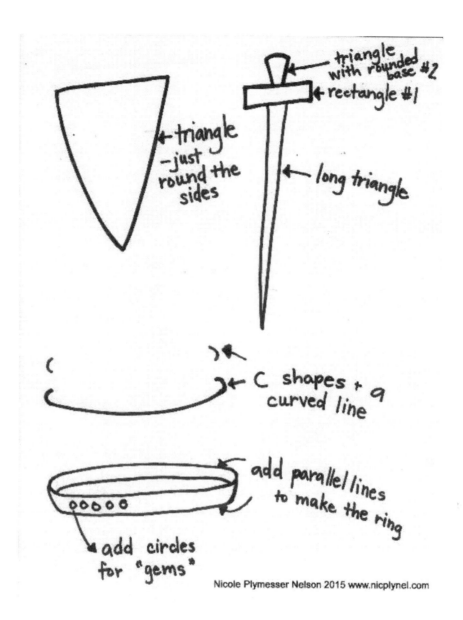

triangle with rounded base #2

rectangle #1

← triangle
–just round the sides

← long triangle

← C shapes + a curved line

add parallel lines to make the ring

add circles for "gems"

Nicole Plymesser Nelson 2015 www.nicplynel.com

3. I penciled in the rest of the words.
4. I used watercolor to paint a wooden shield, a silver sword with a ruby gem, a golden belt with emeralds. I added the gems to be slightly more royal, but not fancy.
5. I used blues to paint the background and added light washes of purple to give the whole thing depth.
6. Colored pencil scribbles help add to the highlights and depth.

take up the

ARMOR OF GOD

Ephesians 6:13

that YOU may be able to withstand in the evil day, & having done all to stand

New Identity

By Deborah Ann Belka

Once I thought,
myself I knew . . .
but then came Jesus
made all things new.

He took my heart,
made it His own
then my life . . .
He began to hone.

He put into me,
His own likeness
opened my eyes
to all the darkness.

He gave me hope,
when I had none
filled me with peace
when He was done.

Now I am in Him,
He is in me . . .
the True Light
I now can see.

With Jesus I have,
a brand new identity
that will be with me
for all of eternity!
~~~~~~~~~~

Bonus Art Tutorial for Cover Image

When Leslie decided to name this study new beginnings, I was also in the middle of a plant unit with my homeschooled 7th grader. So my brain spun to vines and leaves and new plants sprouting forth. In my imagination I could see the new plant in the early morning dawn light pushing up through the garden dirt and turning toward the sun.

1. I created this with watercolor. I wet the entire piece of paper (to the point of being shiny, but no puddles) and then pooled the different colors on the page letting them bleed together a bit in a few places. Use mostly yellow, then a bit of orange, pink or very watered down red, and then just a bit of purple.

2. When that was dry I penciled in the vines, leaves, and the words. You can write new beginnings or you may choose to put in a word for the year to direct you.

3. You will see the directions on how to draw below:

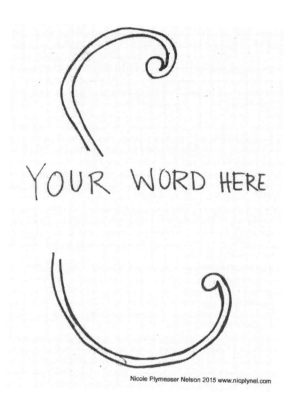

YOUR WORD HERE

Nicole Plymesser Nelson 2015 www.nicplynel.com

4. The vine is just simple curved lines that end in a circle. The leaves are fairly simple shapes, some with pointed tips, some rounded. I then filled them with a variety of lines, shell patterns, or circles.

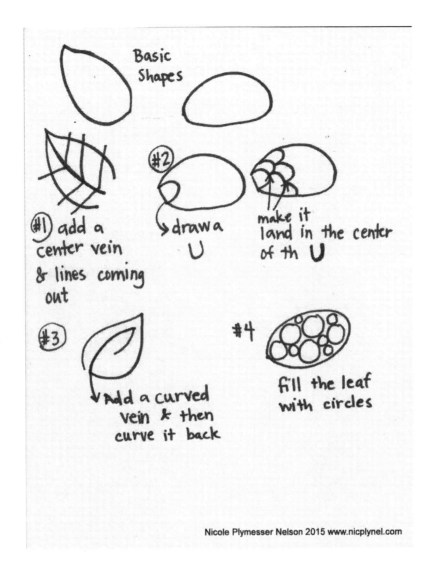

Basic Shapes

#1 add a center vein & lines coming out

#2 draw a U

make it land in the center of th U

#3 Add a curved vein & then curve it back

#4 fill the leaf with circles

5. After they were drawn in I used a variety of green colors to fill them in. Try mixing 3 different shades of green by adding blue or yellow or red.

6. When that was dry I went over the entire design with black marker.

7. Finally, I used colored pencil to make scribbles in the background-covering each area with a like color (pink on pink, yellows on yellow, etc.)

Small Scripture Art for Tracing

THANK YOU!

We hope you learned from this study and grew in your knowledge of God's LOVE for you. Thank you so much for supporting our ministry!

Bible Stories from the Heart creates <u>Adult Coloring Bible Studies</u> that help women read and understand the Bible so they will draw near to God and experience His indescribable love in a new, intimate way.

Our studies feature engaging lessons which include; *Bible History, Word Studies, Reflection Activities, Discussion Questions, Art Projects* and *Coloring Pages.*

<u>If you enjoyed this workbook, we hope you will try some of our other studies.</u>

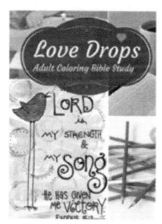 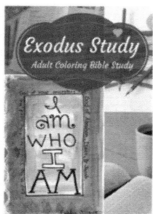  

If you haven't already done so, please join our **Bible Stories from the Heart** group on <u>Facebook</u>. There, you will join a dynamic, supportive and highly engaged community of thousands of women who participate in our studies and post their artwork to share with other members.

You can find more information on our ministry at: <u>biblestoriesfromtheheart.com</u>.

We would love to hear from you! Please feel to reach us by email with any questions or comments you might have: <u>info@biblestoriesfromtheheart.com</u>.

Thank you!

40299952R00063

Made in the USA
San Bernardino, CA
16 October 2016